BOTH SIDES OF THE HEART

POEMS BY REX HOLDREN

<u>BOTH SIDES OF THE HEART</u>

Contents

A Note Before You Start

The first section of this book is dedicated to those who struggle with life. Those who feel as if they live in the darkness. If you struggle to find the light, even when the sun is brightest, I want you to know you are not alone.

So many amazing people never feel the warmth and compassion of others. Sometimes it is the environment in which they live, and other times they don't allow ourselves to feel the love.

Sometimes we are our own worst enemy, as we become our own biggest critic and obstruct ourselves from finding happiness in life. Whatever the case, we struggle with finding our smile, our happy place. We put on a happy face for the world to see, but we are dying inside. We want so desperately to cry out, to be heard, for someone to rescue us.

These poems are for you; for those who suffer in silence, those who cry when nobody is there to hear us. If a sad song or movie has ever made you cry, you will relate to the content of these pages. If you read these poems and feel like crying, do it. Don't feel bad for feeling bad, and don't ever give up on yourself.

You are never alone and you never have to feel unloved. God is with you and he loves you. I am also with you; I have been where you are and have fought similar battles. I won't pretend to know what you are going through, only that I know your pain is real.

SECTION 1

THE DARK SIDE OF THE HEART

The Dark Side of the Heart

In the abyss of mankind's soul,
farthest from the light,
is a place where few recover
when they've lost the fight.
The walls go up quickly,
the surroundings turn cold,
it's a place where nobody is safe
be you young or old.
Though it hears the many messages,
from voices up on high,
it disregards the sights and sounds
for surely these are lies.
It fights only for itself,
no specific gender, race or creed;
very few who've won the battle
learn what it's like to be freed.
It knows everything about you,
and attacks you when you're weak;
deceives you as you share life's waters,
then drowns you in the creek.
Many bring their special weapon,
but it only fears the light,
it will take all you have to offer
and send it back with all its might.
It's not a castle wall I speak of
or a moat that keeps us apart.
It's the wounds we left unhealed
that strengthen The Dark Side of the Heart.

The Pain of a Poet

A person of many words should be able to easily describe
What they feel when the pain is hidden deep down inside
One might think the poet has grace that rolls off a golden tongue
But sometimes the pain is so deep, he just wants to hide or run
Sometimes the poet cries for long hours in the dark
Shutting down all that matters to him, his mind, and his heart
Sometimes the pain arrives without any prior notice
Prevents him from loving, prevents him from closeness
There is no way to describe how frittered and how frayed
So he takes the love given him, and pushes it away
It's hard to accept, when he believes he's so unworthy
No entry to heaven afforded him, he's condemned to live earthly
The pain of a poet described, taking you start to finish
Now that the pain has started, it will never diminish

Taken by Surprise

What do you say when taken by surprise?
Can you find the right words if you really, really try?
Should you let the tears fall, stopping at one or maybe two?
Or should you give each a hug, thinking "That ought to do."?
Will you stop and reflect on the moment at hand?
Or will you speak without thought from the spot where you stand?
Can you accept the kind gifts, and the words that will follow?
Can you stay humble and silent, take your pride and then swallow?
Is it derogatory to be surprised by the kindness you see?
Is it self-destructive to ask in silence, why me?
If your time ended now, on this generous moment,
Would you thank all for their kindness, considering this
bestowment?
Who are you really that deserves such attention?
Just one of so many who are too many to mention.
So how do you say thank you when you are so deeply moved?
You pray silently for each with a love that's not moved.
You remember them all as you drift off to sleep,
Asking God to protect all as a reward they have reaped.

Never Apart

It's been said many times
"Everything is on its way to somewhere else."
But when someone dear departs from us,
they're more than memories on a shelf.
For as long as I have one last breath,
One beat remaining in my heart;
Not even when God takes you home,
will we ever be apart.

Where is the Heart?

Where is the heart? I already know.
I feel its pain each day as it grows.
Where is the mind? It's not hard to locate.
It causes great anguish inside, each time it rotates.
Where is the light, when surrounded by dark?
Punching a hole in the darkness, can you hit the mark?
Where is the warmth of human compassion?
Do you hand it out to some with the smallest of ration?
How does the blood that flows in us all
Not connect us together, the large and the small?
How do you look deep in their eyes
When all you can say is half-truths and lies?
Where is the laughter and why can't I smile?
Why do you hurt me with words that are vile?
Where is your soul? I know where mine goes.
With my brothers and sisters, above the rain, wind and snow.
Who is your messenger, what words will he speak;
Will he fill your thoughts with hatred, convincing the outlook is
bleak?
Where is your hope? Join me and see.
Share an eternity of happiness where all can be free.
'Where has the time gone?' we wonder with age.
First we're young, then we're old, then we turn another page.
We wander through timeless existence, be still we check our watch
Failing to realize time is a human creation while hearing tick-tock.
It's not about how we start this life but more about the end,
And all the things that come in-between is what pays the dividends.
It's not how you look, your money, or life that's filled with pain,
It's about being who you are while standing in the rain.
Will you buckle to peer pressure when surrounded by the crowd,
Or will you stick to what you know is right and defend the truth out
loud?
Can you be the one to extend a hand, and pull someone back up,
And help them to see the difference between bad decisions and bad
luck?

Or do you believe there's no such thing as one who has all the
breaks?
Can you tell the differences between the real people and the fakes?
Do you believe in destiny with a predetermined plan,
Or is free will embedded in you, so you take all that you can?
What is it that you call a gift? Your family and friends,
Or is it the material things in life that satisfies your ends?

Is it good enough for you just to be thankful for each breath,
Or does it take gold and silver to keep you happy until your death?
And once you're gone, will you be rewarded for the difference that
you made?
Or will you come back again to correct your errors, and in new life,
offer aid?
The choice is yours, for how you act with each day you exists.
Then you'll know your true value by how much you are missed.

More Words to Come

This will be the first one, with many more to come
That's an often used phrase, so we'll see when then next one is done
Getting down the first word is not the hardest one to write
Many times I've struggled to continue, but the words eventually take
flight
Some call it a talent when they read the words upon this page
But how it reaches down inside you, only you can truly gauge
Mostly when I write, it's from the inspiration of another
Trying to heal the pain inside, trying to recover
Trying to lift my spirits from the darkest, deepest pain
Trying to give my heart a shelter to and dry it from the rain
And even as the last word is inked I still may feel imprisoned
I know there is hope for all because he died for us, then risen
No earthly tomb can hold our soul, no earthly bonds secure
Because he gave his love to all so the darkness will not endure
So as I finish with these words and thank you for your gift
Know I could never do without the love you all have left me with.
It may be me who writes these words with many more to come
But without your love to give them meaning, the message comes
undone

All That That Implies

The day is so cloudy and so full of rain
We're aging so quickly, our bodies in pain
We stare out the window, no sun on our face
Searching to find what we call our happy place
It seems so awful, here where we're at
Trying to hide behind glasses and under a hat
We wish we could find a place where the sun shines so brightly
With a cool ocean breeze, watching the sunset nightly
Sitting in the lap of luxury, living the great life of ease
With no one to make happy and only yourself to please
The truth is you could have everything, and still be unhappy
So instead you are angry, thinking others are sappy
So for now, you'll keep all the days long
To where I no longer feel like a rat in a maze
There is hope for the future and all I desire
But for now, I'm still stressing like my backside's on fire
In closing, remember this small piece of advice
Do whatever makes you happy, and all that implies

Evil Beauty

Only now do I realize my misjudgments and mistakes
Enticed by outward beauty but the heart I did forsake
To lift the cloak of darkness — was it mystery or madness?
Knowing all along it was always heartbreak and sadness
I tell myself each time, that it is time to turn the page
But I make the same mistakes no matter what the age
I can't resist her whisper, it always draws me nearer
I travel out of my dimension, being pulled into the mirror
I don't know how to stop myself, so I brace for the impact
Drawing out my soul and leaving an empty shell intact
When she's through with me, she pushes me back into reality
And like a frightened little child, back to my world I will flee
In the distance I still see her as she takes another victim
Using the same old tricks she used on me is how she will trick him
She never seems to age and her deceits all stay the same
She ruins many lives and she never takes the blame
This is not a woman that I am documenting here
It is mankind's lust that holds us all in fear
We are told that this is pretty, handsome, or attractive
To be sold a way of life that is really radioactive
We don't need to be anyone other than who we are
We don't need giant houses or really expensive cars
All we need is to be ourselves and treat each other well
And know that beauty arises from deep within your shell

Heaven's Not That Far

Many times, I considered ending what I thought was my miserable
life
So much to endure; the aches, pains, loneliness, and endless years of
strife
I tried it once, did not succeed, and thought, 'This is one more
failure'
The next time I tried, I would pass the test, of this I was so sure
Convinced I was not needed, this planet with one less man
But God said, "You're not ready yet." He still had a plan
I would go and live a life that was full of tests and trials
I would feel the pain of others but give them many smiles
I could use my own life, giving examples to many others
Bringing joy and hope to so many, my sisters and brothers
I learned through God's eyes that we are all connected
So repair the hurt, leave the smiles, your tears are all collected
I am not better than anyone, so you will always see me humble
Also, I may need you to catch me, just in case I stumble
Someday we will be rewarded, a life without the pain
And all our crying will disappear like teardrops in the rain
So take my hand, we'll declare happiness, 'God knows who we are!'
And leave the darkness and pain behind, heaven's not that far

If We Could Only Make Believe

I've tried so many times to make a home inside this place
I've closed my eyes and ears, and lived through this disgrace
Endured a life of sadness, disappointment, anger, and fear
I've locked the door behind me, and in solitude let go the tears
When I've let go all of my anguish and gathered up my strength
I'll remove myself from darkness and keep the world at arm's length
Those who share these four walls call themselves my family
But considering how they use that word, it sounds more like
profanity
They see the pain they cause me but if it's not physical, they don't
care
They can see the body hurting, but what's on my mind I no longer
share
All my life I've been told, "Be a man, be tough, and suck it up."
And now everyone seems really surprised, when I lose it and blow-
up
It used to take a long time for someone to get under my skin
Now it is a daily occurrence, happing time and time again
I see the anger in them and I've tried to cure the hate
But they hear only what they want to, and never see their fate
If you read this and understand, try not to be like me
Let go of the anger, move on to love, and let God set you free

Back to You

Nobody else can have their day
Or their moment in the sun
Why do I even talk to you?
You make me feel so dumb
If what I had was good
You've had something better
The next time I talk to you
I think I'll send a letter
If I need to catch you up
I can think of nothing better

So here are samples to start us off
Let's see what you have to say
It will be a one-way conversation
I'm sure it will not keep you at bay

When I was sick, you were sicker
And that really makes me sad
It shows you think only of yourself
And for the rest of us, that's too bad

When I was injured you recalled
The time that you hurt worse
I guess the only way for me to win
Is being driven by hearse

When I was feeling really sad
You said, "I know just how you feel"
Showing you're the one and only
Whose pain is oh so real

So ending this, I'm telling you
That I am more than done
With one exception for you
A prayer to the father and the son

Can I Write What You are Feeling?

You look at me with sadness hidden behind your smiles
Your tears not seen but left behind, a path I walked for miles
The cries for help are silent but to you they are the loudest
You feel invisible and all alone in a room that is so crowded
What do you want, what do you need, can you find the words to say?
Does no one help when you beg and plead, nor God answer when you pray?
Can you find the words with ink and pen to express what you are feeling?
Would the words take flight, and lift you up to a world of love and healing?
You tell yourself that it's your fault you live a life of pain
You wonder if the sun will shine or will you forever walk in the rain
But what if I asked you, "Can I write what you are feeling?"
Would you tell me about all your pain, or would the truth be too revealing?
So here we stand, face-to-face, opposite side of the mirror
Realizing the person looking back at you sees the reality so much clearer
Yes, I am you and you are me, in this same place and time
I'll help you and you help me, up the steps together we will climb

Not Worthy

I feel that I'm not worthy, I can forgive you but not me
My mind gives me reason after reason, it's all that I can see
The brain has control, sending non-stop negativity to the surface
I try to bargain for sympathy but it's too costly to purchase
I look to the sky, but all I can see is the rain
I wipe the tears from my eyes, but all I can feel is the pain
I ask myself, "Why do you care so much for others but less of
yourself?"
My answers betray me: "Life is an open book, but I'm stuck on the
shelf."
I tell myself life is serious and not some game to be played
Again, my mind laughs at me and by my own I'm thoughts betrayed
I look for an ally, and opening my heart, we search for my soul
But the mind has the upper hand, having placed us in such a deep
hole
My heart begs the mind, "Please show mercy, please set me free."
My soul screams in agony, "Don't forget about me."
We are convinced there is only one way out, a choice we must make
We look at so many options but there is only one step to take
It's time for the heart and soul to take control, they conspire for
mutiny
It's a victory of sorts, but comes with much scrutiny
When the heart rules the mind and the soul stands next in command
The life of negativity goes from destructive to grand.
So I'll let the heart take over and pull my book from the shelf
And give a second chance at happiness to someone who deserves it:
myself

She Thrives on Chaos

Strolling through the darkness, hiding from the light
She'll take another victim and fade into the night
Her thirst for blood not satisfied, she'll go out to hunt again
She thrives on chaos, seeks destruction, and feeds upon your pain
You can run and you can hide. But once caught, she seduces
She's caught many in her traps and snares, still hanging in their
nooses
She leaves most of the dead on show, but a few she keeps private
They're still alive for her to play with; somehow they survived it
She holds them captive, possess their mind, and strips away their
soul
Now they're just a wandering spirit, on an endless path they stroll
A few have found their way out, though their story's that of lore
They describe all of her evil-doings. The images chill me to the core
Some day she will look for you and prey on your emotions
You'll be at your darkest moment, your life filled with commotion
And though you may escape her clutches, she will always leave her
mark
Never to be yourself again as she steals your inner spark
So take these words to heart, my friend, and learn the worldly truth
Today has ended and yesterday is gone, just like our days of youth

Why Do You Need Me?

Why do you need me? I'm no more unique than you.
Although I do realize that one is better than two
Why do you need me? You treat me as though you don't.
I want to run and hide from you, but we both know I won't.
Why do you need me? I bring nothing of value to the table.
I have no stories to share that have been put in lore or fable.
Why do you need me? I'm nearing the end of my life cycle.
I'm not an archangel with a name like Gabriel or Michael.
Why do you need me? I cost you more than I am worth.
I've only been a drag to you from the moment of my birth.
Why do you need me? Someday you won't remember who I am.
Mostly you act as if you don't know me, or don't give a damn.
Why do you need me? Am I the only one who will let you scream?
Would you still shout if I told you how it leads to my bad dreams?
Why do you need me? Is it so you have your own whipping post?
If you precede me in death, will you haunt me as a ghost?
Why do you need me? Am I the only one who can help?
Does it reenergize you when you scar my body with your belt?
Why do you need me? Do you live to get the best of me?
If I died tomorrow, would I take the abuse with me or be set free?
Why do you need me? I've asked myself more times than I can
remember.
I pray that someday the spark that is my life burns down to an
ember.
Why do you need me? It's obvious to me I don't want you.
Will I ever escape the person standing here, or is there nothing I can
do?
Why do you need me? Will I get my answer as my ending draws
nearer?
Or will I forever stand here hating who I see looking back in the
mirror?

Rough Day

I think this is going to be a rough day, my mind is all over the place
Leaving my body behind, my spirit is transported deep into space
I have completely lost my focus and I can't control my emotions
No answers to the easiest of questions, no access to a magical potion
This has really become a rough day. Is there no one to help me?
Has everyone found their own way out or have they been set free?
Where is the key I seek? Without it, I can't unlock the mystic door
The one that has held me captive and will forever more
The really bad day continues, and night has yet to follow
Cold and loneliness encompass me, the world has left me hollow
There is nobody I can hold onto, I can't feel a warm embrace
There is nobody I can talk to, no one who speaks face to face
The really bad day has turned into night, leaving me in silence
It grasps me tightly, laughing at me, begging me to be defiant
A childlike dare pokes and prods, pushes me towards the edge
Screaming silently for help, make every promise, every pledge
The really bad day that turned into night has fallen into darkness
Laughing at me as it weakens me, telling me it was all harmless
I struggle with my final thoughts before the covers go over my head
Where does the bad day go, when it's time is up and it's fled?
Final words to my really bad day, in my dreams I am safe as I pray
I close my eyes, tightly fold my hands, thank God for allowing me to
live
As I fade off to sleep I realize I still have so many things to give
Good night, bad day—I'm not afraid of what you can do
Return when the timing is right, and I'll do whatever you choose

What Hurts the Most

If I could change one thing in you
I would change how much you hurt me
It would feel so nice to walk away
Feel the euphoric touch of being free
But what it is that hurts the most
I can't seem to pin down
I don't know if it's you or me
We're lost and then we're found
I don't know if it hurts the most
When you say you'll show and don't
Or things you promise me you'll do
Even though I know you won't
Is there any difference
Between the truth you tell or lies?
Is there any difference
Between what you expose or what you hide?
Can you convince me now
After all these years have past
That the changes you say you made
Are really going to last?
What hurts the most I'm just not sure
The door you slammed upon my face
Or the one you opened
That hid the empty space
Could it be what hurts the most
Is the love you say you have
Then you turn your back on those in need
Because things went a little bad?
It might have been what hurts the most
Is how you left me an empty shell
A hollowed-out tormented soul
To endure a personal hell
I am stronger now than I once was
Thinking back on all those times
My conclusion about what hurts the most?
The power to stop the hurt was really always mine.

Four Seasons of Life

Looking at the pictures brings memories from long ago
Like building people made of snow
Summertime's never long enough, the months pass way to soon
Evening walks together staring at the moon
Spring was a time for love as the flowers began to blossom
Changing colors in the autumn, absolutely awesome
The four seasons come and go, leaving a metaphor for life
Birth to death and all between; happiness and strife
If I could choose one season to live in, that choice would be autumn
Like you, the beauty and the color never to be forgotten

The Dream

Sometimes it feels like I'm standing in the rain
But it's not water drops I feel, it's sorrow and pain
Nothing ever turns out like I wished it would
Leaving this world far behind if only I could
Torn between leaving behind the ones that I love
Or ascending into heaven on the wings of a dove
There is a battle that takes place, it's splitting my brain
One side wants to end me, the other wants me to refrain
I wish I could silence the voices and make the images fade
A peace of mind I'll never get back is a heavy price to be paid
I look for any distraction, and dreaming just won't do
I wake from the nightmares screaming for you
You're nowhere to be found and I'm lost in the mist
Too many days gone by and opportunities missed
Once the mist clears, how will I right the ship?
Can I hoist the main sails and take the rudder in my grip?
Fear sets the course set for my journey, brings the horizon into view
Disappointment comes in waves, sinks my ship deep in the blue
Swim towards the surface, no life raft in sight
Now running from monsters on the ground and in flight
Anxiety holds me in place, but the sunrise pulls me out
Drenched in my sweat, I wake with a shout
The dream is no different than my waking reality
With the exception that one day I will face my finality

It's Not What You've Done for Me, It's What You've Done to Me

Money is the easy part when you have a little to give
But it takes more than paper and coin if you really want to live
Maybe nobody ever told you that 'I love you' goes a long way
Maybe you'll learn to say it, now that I've gone away
It takes more than a roof over the head and food that fills the belly
It takes kindness and compassion, and not a day that's filled with
yelling
It's not about the birthdays or any Hallmark holidays
It's about talking to me calmly when you see my nerves are frayed
It's true, you made sure I had a place to live and plenty of food for
eating
It's also true I endured your wrath, memories filled with
punishments and beatings
I may not have lived under a bridge or begged for money from a
stranger
But the people you exposed me to, all too often exposed me to
danger
I learned much about hate and anger and about what love is not
From watching all you've done, and believe me, I've really learned a
lot
Your abuse covers the spectrum, from the physical to a poison pen
Your cruel vindictive methods change nothing and you will do them
again
It's now what you've done to me that always brings the rain
No matter how you've helped me, I will always recall the pain

The Accident

I use to think that if I had an accident
I would rather die
Than to do something as restrictive
Like wear a helmet when I ride
I would rather have had it ended
In one quick tragic blast
Than to live with the reminder
Of a pain that forever lasts
I would rather not have the visions
That repeat frequently in my head
Even if it meant trading them
To be walking among the dead
However, irony is a passenger
As we journey through this life
It teaches us many lessons
In pleasantries and strife
Now that I've had my accident
And spend every day in pain
I realize my original thoughts
Were naive and filled with shame
It wasn't a sudden epiphany
That made me feel disgrace
It was lying in a hospital bed
And seeing the tears on my children's faces

The Offer of Love

They are waiting in the darkness
Just barely beyond the light
They are looking for your weaknesses
Are you ready for the fight?
What weapon will you choose
To take into the battle?
Is it the body they wish to harm
Or your mind they wish to rattle?
Can you launch your own offensive
Striking blindly into thin air?
Or do you hide in total silence
For longer than you dare?
Maybe you are stronger
Than you ever thought you were
And you'll pass quickly through the darkness
Being nothing more than a blur
And when you finally reach the light
Leaving darkness far behind
Will you bring all your baggage with you
Until you reach the end of time?
I have been where you are
Hiding silently in the dark
Praying that those I hold most precious
Will see my inner spark
We have shared so many feelings
And this I know you doubt
But if you put your life in God's hands
He'll help you work it out
He doesn't wave a wand
Or cast a magic spell
He offers you a choice
Between heaven or hell
It's always your choice
The gifts offered from above
So bow your head and raise your hands
And receive our father's love

Senses

Can see me? Can you hear me?

Or are you just too far away?
If I come a little closer
Will you stay or run away?

Can you reach me? Can you touch me?

Or are your arms not long enough?
Are you afraid of what I might discover?
Like you are weak, and not so tough?

Can you smell me? Can you taste me?

Do I leave a bad taste on your tongue?
Or can you not find the words you need?
Or fear that spoken words cannot be undone?

Can you see that I'm not balanced?

Have I no awareness of my space?
If you answered no to these,
Then you must not like my face.

Am I lacking in my senses or have you had your fill?

If my sense of being leaves you unaware,
Then I must work a little harder
To try to make you care

Can we connect consciously or on levels not yet seen?

I've reached across the boundaries, did my best to reach you
But my failure is one that we both share
The price is a friend we never knew

When He Shares and When He Doesn't

Just because he sheds his tears doesn't mean you can defeat a man in battle.
He is more than the sum of his property and chattel.
The tear he sheds may not be his choice to share with you
But when he does, you know his heart is breaking into two.
The time he shares and where he shares it are commitments of his faith.
He trusts you will accept his tears with mercy and with grace.
When he shares and what he shares can be deeper than the ocean,
Filled with love and hate the heart unseen with deep-rooted emotion.
When he chooses not to share, it may have a deeper meaning.
He may be searching for himself, the purpose of his being.
He may be at his strongest or his weakest when he's silent.
It might be he has given up or seeking inner guidance.
What do you look for, what do you think, when he shares the tear upon his cheek?
Are you looking for a chance to ridicule or is it wisdom that you seek?
When he shares and when he doesn't may never be predicted,
For his desire to leave this world behind is culturally restrictive.
When he shares he tells the world, "I just can't be like you."
When he doesn't share his pain, he says "The world doesn't have a clue."

The Need

If ever there was a time that I need me, it's now
Heart beating fast, sweat dripping from brow
The time to recover seems beyond the horizon
I go under the water again and again
The ship's sails are up and the anchor is weighed
Alone on the dock forever is my price to be paid
I jump in the water and swim from the shore
But the water is replaced by a room with a door
The room has no furnishing but a small wooden chair
Moving away from me as I approach, saying "Life isn't fair."
I move towards the door and it moves out of my reach
Telling me "You should have not entered the water and stayed on the
beach."
I keep telling myself not to worry, this is only a dream
But the dream becomes a nightmare with my blood-curdling scream.
As I walk in circles, the chair turns into a mirror
Staring at the reflection, things become clearer
I need to be me not the reflection I see staring back
I can be stronger and fend off the attack
The time has now come to be as strong as I can
To believe in myself and to strengthen who I am
It will be a life-altering battle in time ending never
And losing means who I am will be lost forever
My battle to save myself leaves sweat on my brow
A heart beating frantically telling me, "I need me, now"

Day Turns to Night

Day turns to night and the world turns its page
For me, time stands still in this never-ending haze
I see the world around me and I feel like I'm in hell
Is it any wonder I'm frozen inside my shell?
I listen to the sounds of the planet as we drift forever in space
I have no way of winning when I can't even join the race
I feel the heartbeat of the clouds as they explode with thunder
I shake from their vibrations as I aimlessly wander
I inhale deeply and take in the air, heavy with rain
I pause, anticipating the forthcoming pain
Surrounded by structures filled with people inside
I have nowhere to go, nowhere to hide
Some peek from inside, just behind the pulled curtain
Curiosity gets the best of them, even when the outcome is certain
So many watch while the beatings takes place
Then disappear into the darkness without even a trace
There is no one to defend me, no one on my side
I have nothing to offer, no money or pride
Stripped of my dignity and all that I own
I no longer am me, I'm just flesh and bone
Trying so desperately to contribute to the goodness of life
Being turned away by so many times cuts like a knife
I'm told I'm not like others, who have it all figured out
I need to cast out my demons and remove my self-doubt
What little help is offered comes from confinement and pills
But my demons remain, and gone is my will
To fix the pain and restore the person I once use to be
Would take a commitment of love to set me free
So when I tell you I'm hurting and in emotional pain
Don't run and hide, or guilt me with shame
Know that I am a part of this world with a soul just like you
And still worthy of love even if the world says I'm through
So look inside your heart and find the strength to reach out
And together we'll learn what life's all about

The Darkened Sky

Do you see the darkened night sky
When daylight hits you in the eye?
Do you still believe that it is there,
when you ask and no one cares?
If wings you had, could you fly high?
Could you reach the darkened sky?
If you left to be up there,
would anyone look up? Would they care?
The light we embrace, it hides your fears.
In the darkness of your heart, you release your tears.
You know inside you're not who they see,
they don't see the worry, the suffering, and agony.
You look so happy, bright, and content,
but you know the cost and pain of the life you spent.
When the darkness reaches down and removes the light,
I pray for your sake there is more than just being right.
I pray for your today, tomorrow, and ever after,
and for those left behind when there is no more laughter.
Life is just a blimp on the timeline existence.
Like a drop of rain in the ocean there is no resistance
So when the light fades to dark and the wings now there,
focus upward not down, it's time for a new life to share.
You won't remember what's under you or what you left behind.
All that's before you now is a magnificent shine.
Nobody knows who or what you'll see, but you won't have to hide.
But I hope we will know our true selves when on the other side.

Cheat the Pain

The only way to win is cheat
And lay it down before I'm beat
And to another give my seat
For that's the only painless feat.

The sword of time will pierce our skins
It doesn't hurt when it begins
But as it works its way on in
The pain grows stronger... Watch it grin.
But...

A brave man once requested me
To answer questions that are key
Is it to be or not to be?'
And I replied, Oh, why ask me?'

What is a Family?

What is family?
Is it determined by blood?
Or is it those closest to you, like your lady or bud?
Is it those you were raised by—a mother and father?
And those you raised like a son and a daughter?
Does it exclude the one you call your life-long best friend?
Or any of those in your final thoughts, as life comes to an end?
Does it matter to you because you're such a loner?
You don't care who's out in the world, because you're such a
homer?
Will it matter to you when you take your final breath.
That you were without loved ones through life until death?
What will you think as you float from your body;
That life was a waste of time, useless and shoddy?
Will you look down on an empty grave where you were just laid,
And pray for a second chance as your soul starts to fade?
Will you ask one last question—"Just what did I miss?"
Or will you walk away smugly, feeling completed and bliss?
Remember this one thing before you pass to the beyond:
Anyone who loved you was family, even though you're now gone.

Too Tired

Tired but can't sleep, my mind won't shut down
Spinning faster and faster as the voices get loud
I wish I could open a door and pull out my brain
And grow numb to it all and feel no more pain
What is it like to be in harmony with body and soul
And not feel time fleeting as my heart grows cold?
How did I deviate from God's divine plan?
What must I do to change the person I am?
Would you recognize the changes or ignore what you see?
Or will your prejudice hold me in chains for eternity?
Is there no way out from this darkened abyss?
Will you wait for me patiently in heavenly bliss?

Late Night Update

Ode to the status box—you want to know what's on my mind?
There are just so many questions with answers I'll never find
It's an open-ended question, maybe a curious one at that
I don't think you really care, you're just snooping for some facts
Just four little words is all you have, but much more it does contain
You're asking if I'm happy, sad, or joyous, or if I'm in some sort of
pain
It could be the worst day on the planet or the best I've ever had
Saying hello to an old friend, a sibling, mom or dad
I can sit in utter silence and type away to all you unseen
They say it's social media; it's interesting fun and keen
Sometimes it's like a warm, fuzzy hug from far and wide
Truth is that sometimes it's our only outlet in a world in which we
hide
So shake my hand in person, give me a hug and visit a while
You may find it's so much better in person to share a great big smile
So in your deepest darkest hour, don't hide behind your screen
Step out into the real world and experience all that can be seen

Changes with Age

Another year, another day
A little more tired, a lot more gray
More laid back, casual, and maybe even bored
Growing more in wisdom, and closer to the Lord
Hearing the footsteps of time walking down the hall
Coming for me someday, and someday for us all
If I listen quietly to what life has say
I can hear the voice of God with each passing day
Yes, today is called my birthday, but a death was the gift to me
When Jesus came and died for me, he shone the way to be
Given me a grace that I'm unworthy to have been given
Relieved me of my burdens when to heaven he had risen
Live your life with God, for each day he blesses you
Someday you'll ascend to a higher place beyond the skies of blue
With no more anger, no more pain, and no more tears
No more about worries of time catching-up.
Eternity has no years

Christmas Everyday

T'was the night after Christmas, and depression set in
It's money spent I'll never see again
Leftover goodies and presents that don't fit
Meaningless goodwill not worth a shit
Seated next to me in church, faces I've not seen before
Treating the meaning of Christmas like a Park Avenue whore
You will pitch in a dollar but not all that you have
Thinking redemption's bought cheap, that's really quite sad
If you can find significance for one night, why not the rest?
Treat every day like Christmas, and give everyone your best
Remember the short life of he who sacrificed for you
And be more like him, when you do what you do
So when that time of judgement comes and it's your turn in line
You can leave the world of darkness behind you, and head to the
light for all time

I Don't Want to See

Take my eyes to stop their gaze
And send me down the path of haze
To curse my everlasting daze
To curse my everlasting daze

I give to you my sight and sound
My only gifts that I have found
Without you I wander, darkness abound
To curse my empty lasting days
To curse my empty lasting days

No spirit soars on demon wings
The heart can't awaken from this bad dream
The pain still grows when angels sing
To curse my everlasting blaze
To curse my everlasting blaze

The veil is lifted, the fog is thin
I feel the touch of you again
Forever to share a lasting kin
And feel the everlasting rays

Till We Reach the No More

It's a miserable day and I'm just not feeling right
I tried hard to breath but the bubble is too tight
The darkness is overwhelming and there is no light
I punch and I kick but with a much-weakened fight
I once had the power and I would fight with great might
The mind is functionalist, I've lost all my sight
The battle is over and now it seems trite
Like the bark of a small dog with very little bite
The mountain of irrelevance reaches to incredible height
The journey over the mountain is an eternal plight
Now I look out over the ocean, the washes, with anger and spite
Hearing the tales of the ghost ships and all that they write
The abyss calls to all people, no matter black, brown, or white
To pull us down to the bottom in terrible fright
And waiting below is the armored Black Knight
Pinned with the sword, we struggle through the great blight
Till we reach the No More, having endured Hell's smite

A Universe for Two

When the days roll by, as they continue to do
I bask in the sun's warmth, and think only of you
When the sun gives way to the glow of the moon
I live for the moment of seeing you soon
When the moon gives way to a sky full of stars
I have no more sadness, or emotional scars
When the stars give way to the vastness of space
I live in solitude until I feel your embrace
When the vastness of space brings me home back to you
My journey is completed, fulfilled in my universe for two

Living in the Moment

A lifetime is made up of many moments.
Some moments go by so slowly, you think they will never end.
Some moments go by so fast, they are over before you had time to
appreciate them.
A collection of memories are racing past my brain.
In Technicolor they play in my mind as if they are happening again.
Just bits and pieces with a whisper of sound.
Strung together like a paper chain on a Christmas tree.
When the chain breaks, they will leave, but they will someday
return.
Will I be able to share them, will others want to hear about them,
Will they remember being a part of that moment?
It's sad that the moments won't last forever.
Maybe they do; maybe they are one long, continuous moment. But
it's unlikely.
We have the ability to record the moment, preserving forever, all
that took place.
But what is the relevance of that recorded moment you watch, if you
were not part of it?
Does it guide you? Did it change you? Did it inspire you?
What will you do with my moments? Will you share them?
Will this keep them going forever?
How will the story change when told again?
Will it still be my moment?
Freeze in my mind, oh Lord, the moments of my life,
Those that I share with all of you.

Where Did You Go?

Where did you go when you once were here?
Are you running from the darkness, are you hiding in fear?
We were once the best of friends through thick and through thin.
You are nowhere to be found now my life seems so grim.
Why can't I find you? Why did you run?
The times were the best, by far the most fun.
Now I'm older and sad because you're no longer around.
Life will never be the same. No more smiles, all frowns.
I want that life back, in a time endless loop.
Instead of sitting alone in the dark on my stoop.
I'll never get over you leaving me alone.
The winds of time blow forever, and chill me to the bone.

Fear Tomorrow

Their yesterday's gone and tomorrow will never get here
Today, no reason to hide—but the next day they fear
What's past is no more, and their future unseen
Wash the dirt from their hands but they still won't come clean
The echoes still there of their never-ending screams
The images won't fade from the never-ending dream
What more must they do to put aside all earthly pain?
How can they break the hold of this monstrous chain?
All that was said, will be said forever more
All the doors that were closed, are opened once more
All that can be felt was like a chill from the wind
All the words that were spoken, will never be spoken again
Mistakes they won't learn from, again they'll repeat
They will walk barefoot on ice, but will feel hell's burning heat.
They will come back again and again and again
The misguided young race, human under the skin
Where will they go when the sun loses its glow?
They'll wander aimlessly forever in a place only God knows
Those with the heart that shares both the good and the bad
Will be warmed by the master to share all that he has

Lost Soul

The eyes of the lost soul searches for the light
The heart never tells them they will only find night
They have no body, but they still have a mind
They will search for eternity, but they never will find
They are looking for answers and something incomplete
They will never find the one they must meet
So they wait in the darkness, where time has no meaning
To catch glimpses of light that seem ever fleeting
How do you break free when the cold grips you tight?
How do you break free from the loneliness and fright?
How do you answer the pleas from inside?
How do you stop the tears from the eyes?
So many around you all say the same thing
But nobody knows how to shut off the pain
They all think they have answers as they shout and scream
They all question your reasons, but they don't see your dream
The nightmare is never-ending and it stays wherever you are
It makes no difference if you're near or you're far
Will it follow from this life to each one after that?
Will it show in the light, will it hide in the black?
It must end sometime, when I start life anew
Maybe next when we meet I will recognize you
So keep thoughts to yourself, I can't hear what you say
The voices drown out your words, they aren't going away
Leaving is not optional, we must all leave this plane
But when you transition forward, will you carry your pain?
I think it's been interesting; one up and down ride
I'll remember you always, and look for you on the other side

Poems Instead of Pain

Words on a page truly don't do.
Friends ask, "Hey, are you feeling blue?"
They wonder and fear and pray for the best.
But it's simply a coping mechanism to get things off my chest.
It's been a while since I've written, I've held too much inside.
The truth is I'm happy, and bursting with pride.
It's true there is some sadness.
An inherited madness.
And thoughts rattle around in my brain.
Bringing it all in, smiles and pain.
But what is life, without both sides of the wall?
Hopeless? Meaningless? Maybe nothing at all.
So explore your insides, the good and the bad.
And make room for both, the happy and sad.
You can't appreciate the love without hate.
We would take it for granted, until our name was the late.
So I write this for you, believe it or not,
And I'll finish it off with a wild turkey shot.
So lift up your glasses, no matter what the drink.
Always remember life goes by fast, so don't blink.

When?

When does the daylight touch your soul?
When does a moment cause you to grow?
When a lifetime is at its bitter end,
No more family no more friends.
When is a feeling never enough?
When is the journey considered rough?
When the light has faded from view,
Or sitting in silence wishing life was new?
When is tomorrow going to arrive?
Maybe then you can thrive.
When will day get left behind?
When yesterday has made you blind.
When will your hopes become one with the world?
Will the merry-go-round stop its twirl?
When will dreams end the bitter and cold?
When you realize your heart is tired and old.
When will you stop and relive every mile?
When you open your heart and pull out your smile.

Realizing the Child is Grown

I woke this morning and realized what today was. I cried.
There was no holding back the eruption of memories. I tried.
Images and sounds hit my heart like a hammer made of steel.
Playing over and over, the feelings surreal.
My thoughts drifting back in time and causing great pain.
Moments lost in time, like teardrops in the rain.
Gone forever is the little boy and his hot wheels.
Gone forever are the bedtime stories and colorful pinwheels.
No more running across the floor with his arms opened wide,
Yelling "Daddy's home, daddy's home" when I step inside.

I woke this morning and realized what today was. I cried
There was a man in my thoughts who gave me great pride.
Visions of the future appeared on my wall,
Of a man on his way, walking straight, standing tall.
A vision of great things, so many to come.
We'll share them together, we'll work till there done.
New moments await us, new heights we'll attain.
We've made it through the storm, the lightening and rain.
New adventures are coming and memories we'll build,
With the man you've become, all my dreams you've fulfilled

Can't Let Go of Your Child

From a heart of glass rises a heart of stone
Left to thoughts left all alone
A single smile, a hug and a kiss
Can show your heart all that it missed
The frozen melts, the rock chipped away
Turns sadness to love, every day. I once sat in darkness, cold and
alone
But each time I hold you
I know I am home.
Some times may be rocky
There might be some tears
But I'll hold you beside me
For all of our years.
It's selfish, I know
To need you this way
But I'm so incomplete
Without you in my day.
You are with me always
My thoughts you never leave
And together we share
A life meant to be seen.
I've loved stronger than you ever knew
I'll spend my life making your dreams come true.
All I can offer is my soul and my heart
Which cries out for you
When we are apart.
So I look to the future and beg for you there
A life lived complete, together we share.

You are my heart.

Another Holiday Warped

Easter Sunday, here you are
With chocolate bunnies and candy bars
With colorful baskets and fake colored grass
And marshmallow duckies, what a pain in the ass
Colorful plastic eggs that come in two parts
Contains a variety of candy; some sweet and some tart
A candy maker holiday—hiding behind religion, so it seems
Making us fatter and fatter, making us buy bigger jeans
So the textile makers love these days just as much
As the pharmaceutical companies, and such
We'll forget the real reason to celebrate the day
Because we don't have the courage to be locked in a cave
Remember the real meaning of today, and every day that does follow
As you stick all that junk in your mouth and then swallow

There is Always Hope

It is not always easy for those of us who deal with our own personal Hell. It is true that each of us live with our own issues. Some people are more capable of handling the stresses of day to day life, while others can't find their way out of the darkness. I have come to accept the darkness not as an enemy, not as an ally, not as evil or good, but as the place where I can let go of my emotions without ridicule. It is the place that I now take myself willingly and allow myself to be lost intentionally.

There is a danger that I may not find my way out, but that is where faith comes in. I am a Christian, I am strong in my faith, and I have a close personal relationship with God. We may share the same faith and we may not. What is important is to believe in something greater than yourself. Regardless of your sense of spirituality—whether you believe in my God, your God, a Goddess, or no higher power—we share this time and space together. Even when it feels like the world is against you, you are not alone.

I've lost friends who have struggled to find their light and gave up the pursuit. I have attended their funerals. I have also had friends who are still fighting the fight. I am in that category – I fight the fight. I have friends and family, children, and my relationship with God, but that doesn't mean I've won my battle. There is so much to keep fighting for, and so I battle on. Pandora's Jar may have been closed with hope still inside, but that doesn't mean we can't take a hammer and break the jar open. There is always hope.

There is Always Hope

You've read so many pages and life seems to fade to dark
But you can strike the match that ignites that inner spark
You are more than anything that anyone has ever seen
Your life is an amazing story and you're the star up on the screen
Although you may be surrounded by darkness, you are not alone
There are those around you who reach out to bring you home
The hand that's reaching for you has been in darkness too
So many try to find the light, far more than me and you
So you help me and I'll help you, and the darkness we'll defeat
As we walk in to God's light with a heart that shares a beat

SECTION 2

THE BRIGHT SIDE OF THE HEART

The Bright Side of the Heart

It is true that there can be no light without the dark, and that the darkness is always outside the light, looking to creep in. However, life is so much better when you make it about the love, the giving, and the happiness.

It can be difficult to work your way through the darkness to reach the light. May this section offer you hope and happiness. I pray that you will find at least one poem from the next section to bring you back into the light. If you don't, try to at least find some happiness within yourself. Choose to be happy, choose to love yourself, and if all that fails, remember that I love you and God loves you.

Bright Side of the Heart

It has been said there can be no light without the dark
And sometimes you feel the light is just beyond your reach
So you search for anything you can grasp that won't come apart
Now you find the storm is over, as you walk barefoot on the beach

It's been so long since you have stepped out of the rain
Hand-in-hand, you look deeply into sympathetic eyes
Your heart begins to mend and now you are free of pain
No more excuses, no more denials, no more lies

You feel as if God himself has ordained this blending
Giving you hope for the future for the very first time
A step towards forgiveness, an affection that's never-ending
No more rivers of tears and no more hills to climb

You no longer wait to die. Instead, you pray for eternal life
You dream of riding the clouds with them and your angel wings
You no longer feel the desperation, but pity those with daily strife
As you walk a heavenly path in the sky, where the compassionate
ones sing

All of this takes place without you ever taking your feet off the
ground
A journey you take without leaving home, just take your heart off
the shelf
And realize that the light has been searching for you, and it's you it
found
And the greatest love you can have is a gift from God—to love
yourself

Confession of Sins

I cry for help and confess my sins
Feeling like a lost soul never ends
Whispers of the world replace my voice
To live or die is my only choice
The world spins on its axis, lures me to sleep
I stand out to no one, just one more sheep
I make great effort to change what life is
Nothing is coming for me, it's my time to give
Silently I scream, no words escape my mouth
Spinning rapidly, not east, west, north or south
My feelings attack me, they are out of control
Defeated from the inside and it's taken its toll
I've told you what I need, you say that it's fine
But you never really listen, walking away each time
I showed you my broken spirit and you smiled
With each step away from me, the distance now miles

When Will You?

When you see what the world can be, what do you say?
Does your inner voice convince you to stay?
When you see what the world can be, what do you think?
Does your lifetime of problems suddenly begin to shrink?
When you see what the world can be, how do you feel?
Do you feel like the moment is yours or something to steal?
When you see what the world can be, what do you hear?
Does your heart smile, or beat faster from all that you fear?
When you see what the world can be, what do you reach for?
Do you keep your hand at your side or reach for something you
adore?
When do you stop feeling between a rock and a hard place?
Will you feel that trapped until you've reached your last day?
When do you decide that you have tortured yourself enough?
Will you give into the weaknesses of others, including their lust?
When do you rip open the curtain of your mind and pull back the
veil?
Will you find the shadows on the other side are demons from hell?
When will the last tear fall from your swollen, red eyes?
Will you answer all their questions as your enemy pries?
When you take your last earthly step, in which dimension will you
land?
Will you recognize it and accept it when God reaches out his hand?

For My Love (Mandy)

In everyone's life the most difficult times
Hit hard and cut you deep
You can face your challenges, meet them head on
Or from behind the rock you peek
You can try to run and try to hide
But that's just not your style
There would be far too many hurt
If they never saw your smile
The strongest people are those not alone
And the weakest will fend for themselves
Smart ones will remove bad times from the mantle
And put the good things on the shelves
Sometimes it's difficult to tell
What's good for you and what's not
It's not as simple as putting your hand in the water
To see if the temperature is cold or is hot
Other's think they know what's best for you
And will try to fill your head full of their opinions
But they just want you to fall in line with them
Like you are one of their minions
When times get difficult and become overbearing
I find it's better to find the love in your heart
And share with those who are caring
This brings the story to you, my love
And the future I pray we'll be sharing
It's the simplest of plans, my sweetheart
Not over-complicated or daring
It starts each day
With a wonderful smile
When my thoughts are of you
And a voice without denial
It's a love that grows each day
From sharing our thoughts
And being equal as partners
Our hearts connect at no cost

Sharing our love freely
Being what each other need
No matter how difficult life gets
Together we are freed
So when you think life is rough
Maybe too much to bear
Just call out my name
You know I'll be there
And know I'm always there beside you
To help you pick up the parts
And renew your kind soul
By connecting our hearts
It is my greatest desire
To see you happy in life
Remember these big shoulders
Can carry your pain and your strife
I'll do my best to be for you
The right kind of man
And you'll know that I love you
Each time you take my hand
In closing I'll tell you
The past is the past
And this love that we share
Always will last

Looking Inside You

There are people who see more than we think they do, we call them
'a friend'
They are there from the beginning and they'll be there till the end

They look inside us, and see the happiness and pain
They are our shoulder to cry on, like an umbrella in the rain

Looking inside you, they not only see but can hear
They know the fake smiles when you try to hide your fear

They can feel your heart beating from the movement of your chest
And oftentimes they set us straight telling us what's best

Many times they are closer than your sister or your brother
They know more about who's in your life, like your secret lover

They will protect you from those who would do you harm
And send you towards those who have loving arms

They can also see the happiness that brings about your glow
They figure out what makes you happy before you even know

Who is this special person that makes our love so real?
Our Father above, who gives our life all its zeal.

For My Love Part II (Mandy)

The heart quickens on the long but direct approach.
Stopping, the journey has only begun.
It is a long walk, at least in perception.
The palm sweats and pulse pounds, it can be heard.

It's not as if the visitor had never been there before.
Stopping just before the knock on the door.
The traveler gathers themselves, taking a deep breath.
Slowly the door knob turns and the opening widens.

It's a bright light surrounded by darkness that brings warmth.
The visitor releases a breath, a quiet whisper of a sigh.
It is an eye to eye moment that tells the visitor, 'Welcome'.
It is a touch of the hand that shows the visitor they are loved.

It's not the location that brings the traveler here, but the depth of
compassion
It's not the surroundings that provide security for the traveler, but the
glow.
It's not the history that brings the traveler to the destination, but the
future.
It's not the length of time but the moment that builds the connection.

It is during the beginning of the journey where the visitor hides his
fear.
It is during the connection where fear is pushed aside to build the
bridge.
It is the bridge that beckons the traveler, one step at a time the
confidence grows.
It is the final step—off the bridge and onto solid ground—that says I
am yours.

Surrounded by a wall that no longer is your own, but it surrounds
two hearts.

It is a wall that is built, brick by brick, out of love, and it is capable
of growing.
It is a wall that surrounds the moment, blocks out the past, and leads
to the future.
I am the traveler, take my hand, place your bricks with mine, the
journey is over.

Brand New Day

Rise and shine, people
It's a brand new day
A second chance for you
To make things go your way
Another opportunity
To breathe in the air
Another opportunity
For you to share
Makes no difference
If the sun's out or cloudy
Spend time with friends
Get a little rowdy
Say hello to a stranger
Make a new friend
Tell someone you love them
Again and again
Plant a kiss on a forehead
Or one on the cheek
Tell the world all about you
What makes you so sweet
Take time for the sad one
We know all too well
And drop them a lifeline
And remove them from hell
Remember the hungry
The tired, and poor
Remember our Father
Who loves you for sure
Yes people
The new day is here
Give a smile to someone
And wipe away their tears.

Good Night World

Good night to the world
Until tomorrow I rise
After the darkness has fallen
The new day brings its surprise
The heart torn in pieces
The body submits to its pain
The mind loses direction, then itself
Like tears lost in the rain
Fear tells you you're lost
Hope fades to black
The demons within you
Say you won't make it back
Convinced you are tired and old
This journey is not for you
Outside you're broken
Inside you're blue
But like the day before
The sun lifts its head
And like the day before
Inside you feel dead
You no longer care
If it's day or if it's night
Too beaten to look up
Too discouraged to fight
Here's one last thought
On this hopeless scene
Open your eyes
It was only a dream

Nothing Left to Hide

Here I stand, naked before you
My clothes do not hide the truth
You see only what you want to see
While you put your judgement on me
You make me turn in circles until dizzy
I can't meet your qualifications for living
What can I offer you, beside who I am?
Rejected anyway; I'm not the lion, I am the Lamb
Here I stand, naked before you
Comparing me to all will have to do
No possessions I have to give
Day to day, I struggle to live
I hunger for your acceptance
I'm running out of time and chances
I'm leaving soon, going nowhere
In search of lost loves to share
Here we stand, naked before each other
The journey's over, I've found my lover
She has found me, and together we're one
No more fear, disappointment is done
No more shame, no worries or regrets
No more hearing, "This is as good as it gets"
Leading each other, walking side by side
No longer naked, nothing we need to hide

Every Day

I love you every day
There is truly nothing to make
Sound of your voice, touch of your hand
Create feelings that cannot be faked
It's a love that comes natural
To set the heart free
It's noticed by all
An example to be
There is no taking for granted
To sacrifice comes first
There is no lingering doubts
No unquenchable thirsts
There is nothing as simple
As my love is for you
No questions to answer
Like, "What should I do?"
There are no selfish thoughts
Except how much I need you
Sharing the well of our wishes
How deep and how true
Overflowing with mercy
Forgiveness and grace
I am humbled forever
By the smile on your face
No need to show off
Or try to be more
Happiness flourishes in you
You are the one I adore
Little things add up
Like sharing a task
Or helping when needed
Without having to be asked
It's the little things in life
That matter most to my love
But the best gift I ever received
Was sent to me from above

Rough Start to the Day

When the day starts off rough
As they sometimes do
Just remember
Somebody loves you
When the day starts off rough
And it catches you by surprise
Just think of that special person
Sharing the beauty of a sunrise
When the day starts off rough
And you just want to cry
Lay back in my arms
Feel my heart beat, hear me sigh
When the day starts off rough
And you're too flustered to speak
Feel the touch of my hand
Feel my lips on your cheek
If all the above fails
To make you feel better
Open up your box
And read one of the letters
If the box is not handy
And you still don't know what to do
Just keep reminding yourself
That I still love you

Not Love at First Sight

When I first met you
I may not have known it then
That someday I'd be standing here
With my lady, lover, and best friend
There will always be those doubters
Those who thought that we would fail
But they never knew the depth of our love
Or how we'd walk down the same trail
We've had many years together
Some wonderful and some rough
But if we spent two lifetimes together
That would never be enough
It's amazing how much more I feel
When I hold the three children that we share
Sometimes it's more love than I deserve
When you show me that you care
There has never been a day gone by
Since we've said our vows
That I didn't look in awe of you
And silently said, "WOW."
I may keep those thoughts and expressions
Sometimes deep inside me
But as I read this poem to you
My mind has been set free
You are my one and only
My companion and best friend
And if life ended here today
I'd ask God to join us again

Do You Know?

If only you knew
What I couldn't say,
It would change your life
Day by day.
If my thoughts guided my actions
What things would I do?
Would the words ring out loud,
Or would my actions show love to you?

If you only knew
What I felt each time we touch,
Would you see the fireworks inside?
Would it be too little or too much?
If my response to your touch
Showed compassion and love,
Would you realize the gift
Packaged and sent from God above?
If you only knew
What I hear each time you speak to me,
Would it sound the same to you?
Would each word spoken set you free?

If the sound echoed back to you,
Would it ring out like a bell?
Would you hear that you have set me free,
And delivered me from hell?
If you only knew
How all my senses react to your presence,
You would feel the warmth of my love,
So elegant and pleasant?
If all my senses could bring you
All you have given so far to me,
You would know what I can't say.
You are all I'll ever need.

The Tears in Our Eyes

I held your hand as I watched you cry
We both know all the reasons why

Years go by, memories accumulate
Then life falls apart, can't stop, too late

There is anger and fear, and the feeling of failure
Did you do all you could? You may never be sure

It's a life plan change that leaves you empty and hollow
But I'm there with you, always to follow

It may not be helpful, I've been there before
Like the endless times the waves reach the shore

Your struggle is the only thing, that's all that you feel
But take hold of my hand and you'll begin to heal

Don't stand in their judgment or question oneself
The pain is enough punishment you've given yourself

The hurt will subside, but that's not helping you now
It separates your being, like a field that's been plowed

I held your hand and you watched me cry
You wiped away my tears and we both know why

When one of us hurts, the other does too
It's a connection so deep, the love has to be true

I hurt when you are hurting, but this is not about me
It's about helping ease your pain and set your soul free

You tell me at times I need to be selfish, so that's what I'll do
I'll remind you daily how much I love you

'I love you' may be something you have heard often before
You may have believed them down to your core

I won't compare myself to those in your past
They were missing a love that was meant to last

This may be the first day of many difficult days to come
But when it's all said and done, from you I won't run

You have me now and as long as you want me
For only when I am with you, have I been set free

Remember I am beside you, no matter how dark the skies
And together we'll wipe each other's tears from our eyes

Your Beautiful Face

Night moves in, and our world turns to dark
The daylight retreats, but has left its mark
Laying down beside you, I begin to realize
I need one last long look at those beautiful eyes

The darkness covers us and tries to remove
The images of love, so I move closer to you
The darkness that surrounds us goes on for miles
But I'll drift off to dream about your beautiful smiles

I'll pull you in closer, your back to my chest
And feel your happiness with each taken breath
I can hear your heart beating and I feel both hearts align
We share a rhythm of love that lasts for all time

The darkness may cover your beautiful face
But I remember it well as my finger has traced
When the darkness has past and the sun shines through
The work day may try, but it can't separate me from you

You are my focus and my desire to make proud
On my mind each day, as much as the work day allows
As the work is over and I leave the building behind
It is your beautiful face I seek to find

One more glance, one more touch of your hand
Allows me to be myself, be your man
It's more than physical and more than desire
It's your compassion and caring igniting my fire

You may not see what I see, from the inside looking out
You have a beauty that lingers for me, there's no doubt
So gaze deeply into my eyes and again I will trace
All the curves and edges of your beautiful face

Night is Calling, Eyes Are Falling

Daylight has hung up the phone and night has come calling
Struggles of the day are fading behind eyes that are falling

Sleeping the problems away seems like what we need most
We pull the covers up over our heads and hide from the ghosts

The demons we battle are born from what we think we have lost
To win the war in our mind comes with such a heavy cost

We try to shut off the voices screaming in our head
For that one brief moment we wish we were dead

But the dreams we thought would be nightmares take us to a new
place
Where love grows without boundaries, and you have a smile on your
face

The dream is colorful, with the clearest of sound
It's not a night-time vision, it's you I have found

I pinch myself, to see if I'm asleep or awake
The only thing I feel is anger towards daybreak

I want this dream to last forever, with you in my arms
Lost in your magical touch, held captive by your charms

But now that daylight is rising, and night-time is falling
I struggle to hold onto my dream as the alarm has come calling

With my head on the pillow, and the dream gone from my head
I'm wishing you were beside me, lying in bed

The smile from the dream has faded and I can no longer recall
The events that held me in a restful state of awe.

I take my morning shower, and drive off to my work
I'm pulled back into reality with a sudden jerk

Life itself is just merely a formality
The time I spend dreaming is my reality

Daylight has hung up the phone, again night has come calling
Struggles of the day are fading behind eyes that again are falling

One more dream like the last, nothing else will do
Dreaming is my reality, as it will lead back to you.

The World Around Us

Everybody has something to hide
Intentional or not, things get buried
Sometimes they are pleasant
Sometimes they are scary

Everybody wants you to know
Exactly who they are
You see it on the outside
Their looks, home, and car

Most people confuse sex with intimacy
But it's really not their fault
Society fills us with images we can't live up to
It's like an open wound filled with salt

Most people are in their own little world
Unable to see beyond the road they travel
And the road will get much shorter
As their world begins to unravel

I tell you I have nothing to hide
That my life is an open book
I don't fear the sharing of my past
I invite you to take a look

I show you the extent to which I'll go
But without the worst scenario to demonstrate
I leave the foresight to the world
And my heart to you by fate

You speak as if you have struggled
Terms like 'Avoidance is my coping mechanism.'
But I hear this as if you feel punished
Put yourself behind the walls of a self-made prison

You show me the willingness to love
And with that love comes many smiles
It spreads a joy that warms the heart
As we travel together for many miles
We may only just be beginning
But it is the best of starts
Reawakened by a spiritual love
With the blending of two hearts

We may have many years to go
And could face some unknown struggle
But together we are stronger
And no one can burst our bubble

The Battle

Every day I fight the battle
Of keeping or ending my life
Too little acceptance, too much judgement
Too little love, way too much strife

So many ways to end it
So few reasons to stay alive
I can't soar among the eagles
No wind to carry me high

Still I fight the battle
That seems I cannot win
But still I find the strength
To begin each day again

I'm not sure what moves me
As I walk blindly through each day
Feeling cold and all alone
With not much really to say

I would like to say that I have hope
But I have no truth or lies to tell
I can only hope that you notice
I am living in a personal hell

Most people move past the pain
But I am not like them
I can't confide to anyone
Not family or friends

Nightmares are where I live
Running from life, leaving no mark
The light seems just beyond my reach
I'm cold, alone, and in the dark

Every day I fight the battle
Should I stay or be leaving?
Would my absence be felt
Or would someone be grieving?
If I only knew what waits beyond the veil
I might take the chance, take the step
Leave behind my earthly memories
And every time I wept

The uncertainty of not knowing
Is less scary than what I leave behind
And although the thought is still a dark place
Acceptance, love, and kindness I could find

But for now, I'll take this battle
Day by day, even though I'm losing
Because there are those who love me
So life is what I'm choosing

The battle will never be over
And I may never be set free
But even shackled by the darkness
I'll find the light to lead me

Busy Life

When life finds us busy, and it sometimes does
It's time to stop and look around, just because

A world around us, relevant and irrelevant, but you decide
It's impossible to keep up, but many times we've tried

You wonder what the world offers that you cannot obtain
Is it full of sunshine and daisies, or full of snow and rain?

And if it is full of dreams, are they happy or nightmares?
Are you surrounded by people who would harm, or those who care?

And when life does take a deep breath and slows its pace
Are you frowning, or have a smile on your beautiful face?

Do you often wander, as others go sailing by you?
Do they stop and take a moment to think like you do?

Are we as different from each as an eagle to a dove?
Are we predatory by nature or filled with never-ending love?

When the world goes by so fast, can you see the forest through the
trees?
The wind on your face, is it from how fast you move or a cool
autumn breeze?

Can you put the brakes on the planet and stop the world from
spinning?
And do you sometimes wonder about the game of life—are you
winning?

If you added up all the things in your life and to each one gave a
score
Would the totals point towards riches, the stuff made of fame and
lore?

Or would the riches be more subtle, like a heart warm and deep?
Would you be too busy to know my heart is yours to keep?

Lucky Versus Blessed

I have to sit and wonder because I just don't know why
Being lucky instead of blessed, to find the answer, I will try

When I ask the question, I get a variety of reasons
But to use the word *lucky* seems more like treason

I like to think I'm blessed in oh so many ways
Starting off with you, my love, sharing each and every day

I'm blessed for all the family, neighbors, and friends
And that brings me back to you, again and again

Of all the people in my life who have gone and who have stayed
I have feasted on their happiness, causing my departure to be
delayed

I have drank in all their beauty and been bathed in all their glow
Some I remember in great detail, and some I'll never know
I've heard so many say, "I'd rather be lucky, than good."
But I'll stick to being blessed every day, just like I should

There is no comparison between being lucky and being blessed
If you spend your days relying on luck, your life will be such a mess

I've never been the lucky type but I could always trust in good
That is what brought me to you. Somehow I knew it would

They can keep their luck, and I'll take all the blessing that God gives
Because each day that I get with you, is a blessing to be lived.

The Mask

The face the public sees
Is truly the perfect mask
Nobody knows if you're hurting
Nobody even asks

They see a glowing smile
And hear the laughter in your voice
But the persona the public sees
Is not the one of choice

What they see on the outside
Looking at all the worry lines
They miss the hidden treasure
The one your true love finds

He knows the secret
And only he holds the key
Together, hand-in-hand
Two hearts linked for eternity

So if you're out late one night
And the mask is what you see
Remove the mask and show the world
The love that set me free

When I Wake Up

There are times I wake up
And a morning coffee just won't do
There is something missing
When I don't wake up with you
There are times I sit at work
And things just don't seem right
Then I get a great big grin
Because I know I'll see you tonight
There are times I hear a song
The words tear me apart
Then I hear your lovely voice
And it repairs my broken heart
There are times I see the news
And in the world there's so much pain
There may be storm clouds overhead
But you are my umbrella in the rain
There are times I sit back
And listen to the sounds
Noises of anger, hatred, bigotry
But the love you speak knows no bounds
There are times I wish myself
To be removed from this saddened place
But the thought that hurts me most
Would be to never see your face
There are times I can't remember
Just how did I get hear
But then I think back to when
You pulled me from my fear
There are times when you're not here
And the bed seems so cold and lonely
But then I close my eyes, and I can feel
The presences of my one and only
There are times when I wake up
And I see your smiling face
And I realize how blessed I am
To receive your love, warmth, and grace

When Love is no Longer Free

When life hits you hard
And love is no longer free
Pull yourself from the battle
And share with me the shade beneath a tree

When the oceans of chaos pound your shore
And love is no longer free
Grab my hand and we'll fly
To our oasis, just you and me

When the walls of your castle fall
And love is no longer free
I'll champion your cause
In my armor of love, unbreakable and shiny

When the past haunts the present
And love is no longer free
I'll take you to the future
A place just for you and me

Sometimes love has a high price to pay
Love's not easy, not cheap and not free
But I'll give all that I have
To keep your love with me

I Can't Sleep

I find myself unable to sleep
Laying crossways on the bed
I reach for what was once there
But you are just an image in my head

There is only one explanation
Why these images seem so real
Without you I'm not whole
Without you I can't feel

All alone I've grown so numb
And time passes way to slow
In time, you'll be in my arms
And my love for you will show

But for now I'll stretch my body
Across this queen-sized bed
And hold fast to the thought
Soon my pillow will hold your head

So when the time comes
And you lay next to me
It will surely feel like you're home
And as your body spoons with me
I'll gently fall asleep

When Day Turns to Night

When day turns to night
And the moon is on high
The stars slowly brighten
To match the twinkle in your eye

Planets rotate
As they travel through space
But they can't match the splendor
Of your beautiful face

When the sun finally rises
And we see the morning dew
There is no sight so wonderful
As when my eyes behold you

The Story of You

A long time ago
In a land far, far away
Lived a beautiful queen
Who ruled night and day

All would bow down before her
A willingness by all
Loved by the entire kingdom
Those who were big and those small

She ruled with her heart
And guided by her mind
When all seemed helpless
A solution she would find

Two children she had
A princess and prince, but no king
Although many men would seek her
Offering poetry and a song to sing

None met the challenge
Of what she really did need
She kept hidden inside
Her heart desired to be freed

Before she lost her king
Her heart was imprisoned in the end
But what she needed to be happy
Was a lover, partner and friend

Hiding behind her desire to help
She helped the sick, sad, or hurt
Working with those in age
From near death to birth

Avoidance was her coping mechanism
But the battle to be herself and feel love
Was never-ending and a losing one
Until she received a gift from above
Divine intervention must be responsible
For the injured who fell into her path
He was a saddened old soul
But without judgement in his path

A connection was made
A spiritual bond had formed
She began to feel the possibility
That her heart might again be warmed

She helped the injured man
And he worked hard to recover
But he didn't imagine
That one day they'd be lovers

The queen's old king
Who was cruel with words
And he treated his subjects
Like they were cattle in herds

Many weeks past
And the queen made a good friend
There was laughter and smiles
Her heart was slowly to mend

One day the injured man was better
He left for home but not her heart
With each passing week
They were sad they were apart

Innocent gatherings began to take place
Communication turned to lunches
Each week, meeting with smiles
The waves of joy came in bunches

Many prayers from the injured

To repair the king and the queen
But no healing took place
So the couple decided to break clean

Much guilt was felt by the injured man
He was a man of strong faith
But the more time he spent with the queen
The more love between them would take place

He fought his desires, but she was convincing
Although there were no promises made
She said 'Have no regrets with me.'
Still he felt a steep price would be paid

You see, the injured man had more than a physical break
He struggled with a hurt inside him
One that had brought down the lights
On his love, making his heart cold and dim

But she was a loving queen
And he finally gave in
She was beautiful and kind
He would try to begin again

Daily they showed each other
How great love could be
She was free of her prison
And his heart had been set free

They had a love that grew stronger
Each day that went by
It was a love so natural
The needed not to try

But they showed their love
In the simplest of ways
With cute little pet names
And warmed by love's rays

But time passes quickly

And love's happiest pair
Found a life lived together
Is too short and not fair

They grew old together
And one by one they did pass
But they met up in heaven
Where their love continued to last

But don't be sad by the ending
Even though the story is true
The tale is about happiness
About love and about you.

When Desire Turns to Passion

When she is in my field of view
She ignites my sole on fire
The moment we make eye contact
Kindles the deepest of desire

With each step she takes
My pulse picks up its beat
My body begins to sweat
My passion generates heat

The desire to hold her closely
To feel the touch of her skin
Brings two hearts into harmony
Shakes my stuttering chin

The words won't come out smoothly
I'm getting weaker in the knees
I start to walk her way
But fear causes me to freeze

I want to hold her tightly
And press her lips to mine
In eager anticipation
I wait to catch the sign

Is she looking at my body?
Or is she needing just my time?
Does she share the same desires?
Is passion on her mind?

No matter what she's wearing
Or if her hair's a mess
It's what comes from inside her
A total package, I confess

She is reaching for my hand
And she pulls me to her body
Kissing me very gently
Dear God, she's such a hottie

But I don't see other women
Quite the way I see you
Even though they're attractive
No other could ever do

She tells me all about her day
And pleasantries we'll exchange
But now I pull her to my body
Dying until she's in range

I ask myself, 'What does she need
And what is she looking for?
Does she want a foot or back rub,
Or is she looking for something more?'

I will do the best I can
To fulfil her every need
If our bodies become one
Our stress will be relieved

And if the night winds down
And we fall asleep too soon
I am perfectly happy with the night
If all we do is spoon

So let the night fall down on us
And become just what we make
I'll gladly wait with patience
For I am hers to take

So when she chooses to say goodnight
And the physical was on ration
I'll wait as long as she needs me to
Because soon, her desire will turn to passion

The Silent Battle

Before you read this poem, let me tell you a quick story.

I was raised by my mother and two sisters, I've been married twice, and I have a daughter and two step-daughters. I've watched as both my children were born. I've seen the death of some women very close to me. I miss my grandmothers more than a man my age should admit. With all that being said, I should have a pretty good insight into the mind of a woman, but it only goes so far.

No man has women figured out one hundred percent. Yes, there are some men who have a way of attracting the woman they desire. However, no man knows what battle she fights when she is alone. Being raised by a single woman in sixties in America was difficult. She didn't earn the same as a man, and she faced discrimination when it came to housing, as well as income. She had to rely on friends and neighbors to help raise the kids. She had to drop them off at grandparents' homes at the weekends and summers just so she could work multiple jobs to make sure her children had food, clothing, and shelter.

That was my mother. How about yours? Women are fascinating beings. They have a body that is pure artwork, a spirit that is driven by passion, desire, and necessity. Men are simple creatures. Feed us, show us attention and tell us how great we are, and occasionally indulge us with our desire for physical pleasure. Yes, there are exceptions to both. However, men usually do not hide their feelings to the point where they cry in the dark.

As a man, I can shrug off the issues of the day for something that pleases me more. I know there are the "kick the dog" kind of men out there, but a "real man" doesn't need to commit acts of violence to deal with his frustrations. As a man, I fight my battles—or choose not to fight them—in public. I don't have to hide in the dark when I feel bad. I can choose to get it off my chest or keep it inside; I have that option, a single mother doesn't.

This poem is for the single mothers of the world who struggle to take care of their children, struggle to keep their sanity, and who curl up in a ball and cry when nobody is around. This poem is for every single mother who fights The Silent Battle!

The Silent Battle

She watches from a distance, balancing vigilance, protection,
and giving them space.
She pretends to be happy, content, and blessed,
with a pretend smile showing on her face

Her insides ache from the sacrifices she makes
from putting herself last.
There is no sign of loneliness as her children grow up
way too fast.

She has become a master at multitasking, juggling,
and providing what is needed.
Never having time to step back, and look long enough
at the world she has seeded.

Eating last, and many times alone,
she finds the meal unsatisfying as her eyes well up.
In silence, and staring in to her coffee, she asks herself
"Will I be able to finish the cup?"

Meals aren't the only thing interrupted;
it's difficult to get a good night's sleep.
Lost hours of slumber come from fevers, and chasing monsters
that make the floor creek

Hours spent not her own on homework,
but at some point she has noticed it's beyond her ability.
She does her best to study the subject matter
but she cries, feeling she's lost her mental facilities.

Hours spent coloring eggs, hiding presents, and tying bows around
packages
until her fingers hurt.
Measuring their height one notch at a time on the door frame,
as they celebrate each growth spurt.

Life passes by and you can leave them on their own,
but you worry how they feel when alone.
The worst of your imagination plays repeatedly in your head,
so you pick up and dial the phone

Trust is a hard thing to find.
You have already been let down so many times by so many people.
Your mind drifts back to broken promises,
taking you all the way back to the building with the steeple.

Promises broken are not soon forgotten,
and to protect it, you place bricks around your heart.
You've watched as those you love have lived a life of pain,
and had their world torn apart.

But the children have grown and they are no worse for wear.
It's your time, your turn, do you dare?
Can you put the past behind you, change your solitude into a life
with someone to share?

Life is truly better when
you have experiences to guide you down an uncertain path.
And if things don't go the way you had hoped,
are you under control or do you expose your wrath?

Even God doesn't control everything,
he gave us something called *free will*.
So take some time for yourself, become renewed in life,
and share in the thrill

Woman, you are amazing,
and you have worked your way through the most difficult of times.
So become the person you always wanted to be.
Live life every day for yourself, not just sometimes.

With the passing of time, you now understand
the battle doesn't ever really end, but it doesn't have to be silent.
Live a life of love, and find time to love yourself.
You will soon realize it was time well spent.
Ladies, you are amazing!

Today Has Been So Busy

Today has been so busy
It's time to take a step back and breathe
There are days when I hate this pace
And I wish I could do what I please

I sometime wish I could walk out the door
And leave this place far behind
And join you in a happier place
And stay there until the end of time

If I could build the perfect place
The population would be so much less
Just takes the ones I love the most
And leave behind this earthly mess

I would build a place near the shore
Where by day, the sun always shines
And the cool breeze blows in from the sea
As we walk the beach, your hand in mine

I would build a place with a fragrance
Where the flowers always bloom
At night we would all sit around the fire
And shares stories by the light of the moon

I would build a place, a house so big
A mansion with many, many rooms
A home meant to be shared by all
A home void of gloom and doom

I would get help from all who came with us
So nobody ever feels left out, alone
A place built so warm and beautiful
A place we all could call home

Love is...

Love is commitment
A promise between two
Devotion for all days to come
Joining me and you

Love is trust
A person on whom you can depend
An unwavering faith
Conviction without end

Love is sharing
Hopes, dreams, and fears
Childhood stories
Memories throughout the years

Love is ever-changing
A journey through life's trials
An equal partner by your side
To share sorrows and smiles

Love is forgiveness
Emotions of anger, frustration, and pain
Knowing you're with me always
Nothing to lose, everything to gain

Love is acceptance
Patient, honest, and humble
Loving all aspects of each other
And catching each other when we stumble

Love is eternal
When two hearts become one
The journey is just beginning
The best is yet to come

When Love Comes Back to You

I offered up my love to all of those
Who passed me by on the street
Some smiled, some cried, and some laughed
Walking away, I felt defeat

Those who gave me something in return, called it love
But they pulled it off the shelf
Eventually, leaving me standing alone, angry, disappointed, hurting
And doubting myself

Replaced by the bigger, better deal
I realized the common denominator was always me
Changing who I was seemed like the best idea at the time
But I decided instead to flee

It was easier to trust nobody, including myself
And hide my heart beneath the covers
Pasting a smile on my face and making excuses
Not to risk the love offered by another

The risk seemed too high, there seemed no way to win
I felt unable to begin again
You touched my arm, looked into my eyes
I discovered I already loved you as a friend

You spoke the words "Whatever happens, happens, no regrets."
But I wasn't ready yet
I kept a small distance, but I could feel the bricks around my heart
fall
Could I ever forget?

Could I put myself out there, could I give all I have to give?
Could I win at love or again, would I lose?
The bricks fell and the wall was down, I realized this wasn't the
same

The feeling was brand new

It was no longer a risk but not guaranteed, taking the chance
I kissed you and I began to melt
Each time I would hold you, each moment we would spend together
Your love I always felt

Tomorrow is not promised to anyone, and to love each other
May be the best we can do
We will never feel alone again because this is what happens
When love comes back to you

Virtual Rose

It's 8:30 a.m. in the morning
And the day is well underway
I have been thinking about you
I do that all day anyway

I look forward to the moment
When I'm spending that moment with you
Also remembering fondly
Things you've done, did, and do

I want more of each moment
I am greedy for you
But that's not a newsflash
It's not really anything new

I look forward to old age
When our time is our own
And taking the time
On journeys from home

We have a white board
Full of wonderful trips
I can't wait to start on them
What we don't like, we can skip

But we have to wait
Be patient and composed
So while we are waiting
Here's a virtual rose

It's a very lovely flower
Not your favorite, I know
But was drawn by a hand
A talent to show

Keep it close to your heart
And when you do think of me
Then we'll go where the road takes us
Enjoying what life wants us to see

Twilight

The Twilight of my years, my breaths
Feed the beats within my heart
They tell me there is so much more to life
As I watch the world fall apart

Nerves of molten lava
And pain can go from skull to feet
Collisions sharpen the sensation
But at times it feels so sweet

Darkness mans the outposts
Keeping the light contained within
The prisoners are love and devotion
Behind the barbed wire a sentence that never ends

A heart that tells the vocal chords
Scream and set yourself free
But it only makes a whisper
As the lips and tongue do freeze

An hour passes, maybe two
As you wander within the yard
Then night returns you to your cell
On a bed that seems so hard

There is no comfort on the pillow
The blankets don't keep you warm
Noises unknown echo in your mind
Sleepless nights are the norm

You try to appeal to those who listen
Belong here you do not
Your innocence is not believed
Your name they have forgot

No books to read can satisfy
The food, repetitive and tasteless too
The only spark of hope that's felt
Is the image I hold of you

To be Remembered

He's a gentle man with a heart of gold
She's a gentle woman, their bodies grown old

Spending their nights together, she feels the heat from his glow
He feels a calming sensation from a love they have grown

Too many nights spent a million miles apart
Desires growing stronger by a flame fanned in the heart

Life passes by so quickly, we have so little time
As we search for a treasure, what will we find?

Is it a bag full of gold, or maybe a box full of jewels?
Or an empty box of lost time, so cold and so cruel

Is the treasure a parchment with the story of you and I?
How hand-in-hand we walked, and together we'd fly

Is it a gift we can pass on, something we can't take when we pass?
A worldly inheritance of a great fortune amassed

Will we be remembered after oue story is told or inheritance spent?
With no traces of us left behind, not even a scent

Would it be better to bury it, hoping someday it's unearthed?
Maybe those who would find it, would see the treasure's true worth

Monday

Fasten your seat belt and pull the safety bar down
It's Monday morning, no time for a frown

The work week's like an amusement park with all kinds of rides
Some will spin you around and around and some take you to the sky

Some have many twists and turns, some go a little too fast
Some seem to go on forever, some we wish would last and last

Sometimes the ride breaks down, and is in need of repair
Sometimes the ride is built for just one, sometimes two can share

Sometimes the lines are so long, we wait patiently for many hours
But if you stop and look around, the path to the ride has beautiful
flowers

Eventually the last ride is over as visitors leave through the gate
Where we leave the work week behind for a weekend that's great

So join me on a journey. This amusement park is a blast
Hand in hand we'll go quickly because we bought the rapid pass

Thank you for listening to this man not wearing flannel
We will now return you to your regular channel

THE END